# A Few *of* My Favorite Things Cookbook

MEGAN LYNN

To order additional copies of this book, contact:
Xlibris
844-714-8691
www.Xlibris.com
Orders@Xlibris.com

ISBN:   Softcover        978-1-6641-5288-5
        EBook            978-1-6641-5287-8


Print information available on the last page

Rev. date: 06/23/2021

# Introduction

*Hello & Welcome to my Cookbook! A Few of my Favorite Things! Here's the backstory; Growing up in West Philly, in Wynnefield was like living in the best of both worlds. I grew up on 57th and Woodbine with my mom, grandmother and 4 siblings. On one end there was Saint Joseph University and City line Ave and across the bridge there was Brook, Tustin and all the boys. I was bought up in a protective loving home and the best part about it was the food. I grew a love for food right on 57th Woodbine Avenue. I was born under the Taurus sun and moon why wouldn't I love food? There are so many great times I can remember about my childhood and the simple food we enjoyed; like having sock folding wars on the living room floor with my siblings and the grill cheese sandwiches made in between. Hiding my uncle's keys around the house when he came to visit us because we never wanted him to leave after he came by to get something to eat. Making Texas Teacake cookies as a family in the breakfast room being full of flour as well as our clothes and hair. Countless sleepovers, themed parties, and Sunday dinners on Woodbine but what I like to recall the most is the house filled with food made with love. Most of these recipes in A Few of my Favorite Things belong to me but many are recipe treasures from my favorite family members too.*

This Book is dedicated to my Mom Marla Wilmore

I love you!

I represent you!

I feel very Blessed every day to have you as my Mom!

**In Loving Memory Of Desta Mae Morris**

**Granny I miss you more than I've ever missed anyone in this whole wide world!**

**You were the Head of the Family! You were the Glue that kept us together.**

**We miss you!**

**Missing your cooking has inspired this Book the most!**

**I LOVE YOU!**

# Table of Contents

A Few of my Favorite things for Breakfast. . . . . . . . . . . . . . . . . . . . . . . . . . . . . . . . . . . . .1

A Few of my Favorite things to Snack On . . . . . . . . . . . . . . . . . . . . . . . . . . . . . . . . . . . .7

My Favorite Breading & Seasoning Combinations . . . . . . . . . . . . . . . . . . . . . . . . . .11

A Few of my Favorite Salads . . . . . . . . . . . . . . . . . . . . . . . . . . . . . . . . . . . . . . . . . . . . .14

A Few of my Favorite Dinner dishes . . . . . . . . . . . . . . . . . . . . . . . . . . . . . . . . . . . . . .17

A Few of my Favorite Desserts . . . . . . . . . . . . . . . . . . . . . . . . . . . . . . . . . . . . . . . . . . .25

A Few of my Favorite Drinks . . . . . . . . . . . . . . . . . . . . . . . . . . . . . . . . . . . . . . . . . . . . .28

Fun food facts for Appendix . . . . . . . . . . . . . . . . . . . . . . . . . . . . . . . . . . . . . . . . . . . . .31

# A FEW OF MY FAVORITE THINGS FOR BREAKFAST

I've always considered myself a breakfast connoisseur, I learned and perfected the art of making fluffy cheesy eggs at the tender age of 12. My favorite meal of the day is breakfast. It's really the best way to start your day. Growing up with my mother Marla and Grandmother Desta Mae raising me we always had good breakfast. From creamed chick beef on toast to filling Pillsbury biscuits with stewed apples seasoned with lots of cinnamon and sugar. Close your eyes, imagine being sleep and woken up by the fresh smell of well-done turkey bacon, cheese eggs, perfectly seasoned home fries with cinnamon and sugar toast to top it off. You could literally taste it before you sat down to your plate how all the smells devoured the pours in your nostrils.

Breakfast was the first type of food I started to cook, that's another reason why it's my favorite. My grandmother used to tell me my eggs were perfectly beat and scrambled. I was about 11 years old when I first made breakfast for my mom and grandmother, it was a Mother's Day, 1996. Cooking breakfast made me feel proud and gave me a sense of trust from my mother and grandmother. It was more than just being a reliable and responsible student in school. Eggs are my favorite, I don't think breakfast is complete without eggs. Eggs are a component of breakfast that can even stand alone as its own meal. Take my omelets for instance.

# Fluffy cheesy scrambled eggs

Crack 3 eggs in a bowl or cup
Lightly beat the eggs with a Fork until the eggs become a solid pale yellow color.
Add 1 tablespoon of water
Add 1 tablespoon of milk
Add as much Cheese as desired (Preferably American Cheese/4slices)
Pour mix into a lightly butter pan on medium heat
Mix and Scramble eggs in pan until they are cooked as desired
Lower your heat and Sprinkle some pepper on top

# Bacon makes everything Better Omelets

Crack 3 eggs into a bowl
Dashes of: Sea Salt/Cayenne Pepper/ Garlic powder
Shred in ¼ onion
Dice in ½ tomatoes
Pour eggs mixture into lightly greased pan
Keep heat on 3/4 degree level
Add: 2 slices of Pepper jack cheese
Add: Handful of Spinach
Fold omelet in pan, Flip until each side is to your liking
Top with: Chopped up turkey Bacon/ pork bacon/ beef bacon

# Cheese Please! Omelets

Crack 3 eggs into a bowl
Dashes of: Sea Salt/Cayenne Pepper/
 Garlic powder
Shred in ¼ onion, ¼ green pepper & ¼
 red pepper
Pour eggs mixture into lightly
 greased pan
Keep heat on 3/4 degree level

Add: Cheese – 1 slice American cheese,
 1 slice Pepper Jack cheese, 1 slice
 Provolone cheese
Add: Mushrooms and meat (turkey or
 pork sausage cut-up)
Fold omelet in pan, Flip until each side is
 to your liking
Top with: Shredded Cheddar cheese

From 2005 to about 2012 I would have liked to consider myself a nomad. Or better yet a Gypsy but mother really didn't like me describing myself as such. I first left Woodbine Ave to attend college. I first went to Penn State Berks in Reading only to change majors and move back home to complete my Bachelor's degree at Temple University. Coming back to Philly in 05' of course I couldn't live at home on Woodbine. They were still making my sister have male company meet and greets on the front porch like a preteen. I wasn't 21 yet but I damn sure didn't want to relinquish my newly found freedom and lifestyle I had living on Berks college campus. So my sister Desta (named after my grandmother) and I got our first very own apartment.

I went from Parkside Avenue apartments to 67th and Lansdowne and still ended up right back at Woodbine Ave. Moved out again to a high rise on Wissahickon Ave until having to move again to 40th Brown not being satisfied there I moved to 63rd and Lancaster only again to move back to Woodbine Ave. In 2011, I moved to Manayunk, residing there for two years enjoying the night life on Main Street. After my time in Manayunk was rudely interrupted by the foreclosure of Woodbine, I moved to Allison street right off Girard Ave. Finally after learning how to park and mastering the craft of catching mice in row homes I moved again to my location. I'm pretty sure I'll move again I'm actually planning on being a first time home buyer soon. I'll be moving until I move out of Philly comfortably into a rural ranch home making Chacurterie boards for my visitors. The moral of this story was no matter how many different places I called home, my famous home fries always stayed the same...

# It's no place like Home fries

Chop 5-8 Red Potatoes into squares, ovals, or half circles
Add: 2 diced Onions
Shred ½ Yellow pepper & ½ Red pepper

Dashes of: Cayenne Pepper/ Garlic powder/ Sea Salt/ Old Bay
Topped with: Cheddar and mozzarella shredded cheese and Jalapeño peppers

Last but not least for my favorite part of breakfast. Why wouldn't I tell you how to make those delicious stewed apples in the Pillsbury biscuits I mentioned earlier? I like to call them Apple tarts, these tarts can also be done with peaches and or mixed berries...

## Apple tarts

(Apple Filling)
3-5 Peel Apples (must be peeled)
Chop apples in squares or small triangles
In a medium sauce pan Add to apples;
2 teaspoons vanilla extract

1 ¼ cups white sugar
¼ teaspoon ground cinnamon
½ cup unsalted butter

Pop open can of Pillsbury Biscuits or croissants, Roll the bottom of your biscuit in melted butter, Spread and stretch your biscuit to fill with apple filling, Roll and seal apple filling in biscuit with fork or pressing edges together. (1 cup melted butter)

# A FEW OF MY FAVORITE THINGS TO SNACK ON

Now who doesn't love a good snack, huh?

Next to having my way with a breakfast meal of some sort I much rather prefer just a snack. I was the kid with all the snacks at Gompers Elementary school because I had a packed lunch in an orange New Kids on the Block lunch box and don't forget the matching book bag. I was the kid with all the snacks at Beeber middle school because I was able to go to the corner store before and after school almost like every day. Mr. Pat had the best brown bag 25 cent watermelon candies that I will never forget. The burgers and

cheese fries from the store right across the street from Beeber were the best too. If you grew up in Wynnefield around Beeb you know both places I'm talking about. So by the time I got to high school I was the queen of snacks. I had already been named condiment queen by then at home but we'll get into that later with sauces. I was the kid with all the snacks in high school because by then I had money, an allowance and the White Williams scholarship. So since the beginning of time snacks have been my thing. And here are recipes to my favorite dips to snack on...

# Seven Layered Dip

(From the bottom to the top)
Spread your layer of canned Refried Beans at the bottom of the bowl
Spread your layer Sour Cream
Spread your layer **Megan's Infamous Guacamole**
Make next layer out of 4 diced tomatoes mix with can of Salsa
Cut a whole layer of Diced Scallions (4/5 stalks)
Spread 2 ½ cans of Sliced olives as 2nd to last top layer
Top layer is Mixes of sharp and mild Cheddar Cheeses shredded across the top (lots of cheese)

# Megan's Infamous Guacamole

Peel 2 avocados and Pit the seed
Mash the avocados up in a bowl with 1 small onion with a fork
Season to taste with Garlic powder, sea salt, lemon pepper, red pepper seeds, cayenne pepper,
Steak seasoning and cilantro
Add ½ cup salsa of your choice (I like to use Medium salsa for most flavor)
Stir and mix all together
Squeeze hint of lemon and lime on top of dip and mix one mo' time

# Spicy Parmesan Spinach dip

(Depending on the # of guest serving)
Cook 1-2 boxes/bags of frozen Spinach
Season to taste with Garlic powder, sea salt, pepper, red pepper seeds, cayenne pepper,
Vegetable herb seasoning and cilantro
Wait until water is evaporated /leave to cool, then add to mixing bowl
Mix in bowl
8oz. Square of cream cheese
2 cup container sour cream
Consistency should be smooth, thick, and never runny.

# Bacon Buffalo chicken dip

2lbs-4lbs of shredded chicken
2 tablespoons shredded pepper Jack
  cheese
2 tablespoons shredded extra sharp
  Cheddar cheese
2 cups of Reds Hot sauce
2 cups of Crystals Hot sauce

2 (8 ounce) packages cream cheese,
  softened
½ cup crumbled blue cheese
½ cup blue cheese dressing
½ cup ranch salad dressing
A hint of Cayenne pepper
Fry 4-8 slices of bacon chop it up

Combine shredded chicken, chopped bacon, cream cheese, hot sauces, cheddar/ pepper Jack cheeses, blue cheese/ ranch dressings, crumbled blue cheese, and hint of cayenne pepper on top; in a 9-inch round baking dish set in the oven at 400 degrees for 15-25 minutes.

# MY FAVORITE BREADING & SEASONING COMBINATIONS

I remember nights on Woodbine Ave when my mom would wake up in the middle of the night and cut fresh French fries from any potatoes we had in the refrigerator bottom drawer. She used to leave the skin on like a classic Boardwalk fry and sprinkle just the perfect hint of salt on them when they were done frying. I can remember nights waking out of my sleep for those fries and peacefully going back to sleep after devouring them with her. To this day I may wake up in the middle of the night and make myself some of those same fresh cut fries. That's my favorite midnight snack and personally my favorite starch. I've never been a big fan of rice or noodles. Now there's no special recipe for that midnight French fry snack but here are some of my favorite fried vegetables you may like to snack on...

## Favorite for Frying Chicken

3 cups Flour/ Crushed Keebler Club Crackers / 1 cup of Italian bread crumbs.
Dashes of: Soul food seasoning, garlic powder, cayenne pepper, kosher sea salt, and onion powder and parsley.
(Chicken should seasoned and soaked in buttermilk overnight for best results)

## Favorite for Frying Fish

2 cups of Flour/ 1 cup Louisiana Fish Fry New Orleans Style Lemon Fish Fry /2 cups of Cajun Fish fry / 1 cup of Panko breading
Dashes of: Old Bay seasoning, ground pepper, garlic powder, cayenne pepper, onion powder, and parsley.

# Favorite for Frying Vegetables

My Favorite things to Fry; Fried Zucchini/ Fried Green tomatoes/ Fried Pickles / Fried Eggplant.
(Optional – You can season your vegetable before you start the 3 step process too)
1st Step: Flour and season (Garlic powder/ kosher sea salt/ cayenne pepper/ Steak seasoning)
2nd Step: Beat 2 eggs and ½ cup of milk together with seasonings (Kosher sea salt, garlic powder, lemon pepper, parsley).
3rd Step: Dip wet veggies into seasoned Italian Breadcrumbs for last layer then fry.
Deep fry Vegetables in vegetable oil for the best results!

# A FEW OF MY FAVORITE SALADS

They say always eat your salad first. It helps you digest the rest of your food intake. Here's a poem I wrote about Salads;

Salads are easy, salads are quick, salads keep you thin, while the dressing makes you thick.

Salads are made of green lettuce or spinach, salads should have a balance of sweet and crunchiness.

A salad can be made for dinner or lunch with powerful antioxidants you can even plate salad for brunch.

There are 6 types of salads green, fruit, pasta, bound, dinner and dessert, and I truly see why vegetarians convert.

Salad is my favorite way to eat all my vegetables, Caesar salad with Caesar dressing to be specific there's nothing comparable.

Here are some of my favorite salad combos...

# Cheesy Chicken Caesar Salad

Shredded Cheddar & Pepper Jack cheese
Square cuts of grilled chicken
Spinach lettuce
Cucumbers
Cayenne pepper
Diced onions
Chopped bacon bits
Roasted Herb Croutons
Classic Caesar Dressing

# Grilled shrimp Caesar Salad

Romaine lettuce
Parmesan cheese
Black olives
Cheddar cheese
Grilled shrimp
Sunflower seeds
Creamy Caesar Dressing

# Spicy Kale Salad

Kale
Cashews
Tomatoes
Diced Scallions
Jalapeño peppers
Garlic

(Built in Salad dressing. This combo
  basically makes your dressing.)
Roasted humus
Bragg
Cayenne Pepper
Topped with sliced avocados

This last salad was inspired by my aunt Sharifa I just added some extra spice to it.

Fun fact Sharifa's daughter Alex is my favorite cousin on my Mom's side and best friend.
We spent many days and hella nights eating our favorite foods watching our favorite movies together. Alex used to come to our house and my brother would call her the human garbage disposal. She would come to our house on Woodbine and appreciate every left over we turned our noses up at in the refrigerator. Alex saw early and loved how our family still had Sunday family dinners and holiday family dinners. I must say back then I did not appreciate it as much as I treasure and chase that black family ideal now. My favorite story of Alex is called the Thanksgiving Tumble.

# A FEW OF MY FAVORITE DINNER DISHES

As pictures throughout the book show you, you see how our holiday family dinners were set up. Now imagine the dinner is over the kitchen is closed lights off and the food is packed up. Alex and I had plans of watching one of our favorite movies How High or maybe Baby Boy I can't remember. I do remember us going outside in the back by the garage smoking. After indulging in smoking of course we had the munchies. We went inside and made brand new thanksgiving dinner plates from the turkey and gravy to deviled eggs. With tall glasses of Pepsi to match the meals we headed downstairs to my then bedroom in the basement. I was able to set myself up on couch and start the movie, Alex was not too far behind. As Alex came happily prancing down the steps with her plate and Pepsi something made her slip, a ghost tripped her I don't know but all I saw was the plate and Pepsi fly in the air. There was thanksgiving food everywhere! Turkey on the top step cranberry sauce on the wall stuffing in between the banister deviled eggs down on the bottom step. Pepsi just splashed everywhere, Alex frantically and expeditiously cleaned it all up without my mom or grandmother getting up. Alex yelled to me "come help me!" but I was too high and too filled with laughter and

food to move from the couch. We will never forget that Thanksgiving tumble it's our favorite holiday story to reminisce about.

My favorite thing to make for any holiday family dinner are Deviled eggs. My Deviled eggs are my specialty to dinner like my fluffy cheesy eggs are my specialty to breakfast.

Here's an embarrassing story about me now. The first time I had a boyfriend come sit down to dinner it was a Christmas dinner. Of course I was responsible for the deviled eggs. So maybe this time I put seasoning salt and garlic salt or maybe this time I was nervous and put a little too much salt somewhere or maybe my mom was drunk. The table was set and everyone was seated, the blessing of food had commenced and it was time to eat. Small talk was awkwardly going around the table when my mom screams "Ewe these are too salty!" Like

loud and repeated herself as she continued to eat the salty deviled eggs. She had 2 on her plate. Those deviled eggs were my only contribution to dinner which were my only proof to my new boyfriend that I could cook. With the perception now ruined, my mom had to say how salty the deviled eggs were about 20 times before I had enough embarrassment and removed them from the table. That moment really discouraged me from providing deviled eggs for anymore holiday dinners even though my boyfriend ate the deviled eggs and didn't piggyback off my mom's salty effect. So here's my recipe for my deviled eggs and I promise they won't be salty and you won't be salty for attempting to make them....

# Deviled eggs

(Devil Mayonnaise)
Boiled Egg Yolks put in separate bowl
   from sliced boiled egg (mash to your
   liking)
5 tablespoons per mustard / Regular
   mustard/Spicy mustard
1 Cup of Mayonnaise

1 teaspoons of Cajun spices w/out
   Thyme
Hints of; Cayenne pepper, Seasoning salt,
   Garlic powder, and Parsley
(Add Relish if it floats your boat)
Topped off w/ Paprika

So my mom grandmother and uncle crowned me he condiment queen at the tender age of five or six. When setting the table I was the kid who missed the silverware but always went and got the ketchup, soy sauce, hot sauce etc. BBQ sauce is my favorite condiment. Why? BBQ sauce comes in so many different flavors from hickory to honey. Here's a special BBQ sauce I used to enjoy every Fourth of July. My aunt Lucy threw a Fourth of July cookout every year, they blocked her block off, all the cousins came and visited and ate well. Some of my favorite childhood memories came from those Fourth of July BBQ's. My aunt Lucy is my Pop Pop's youngest sister. I love my aunt Lucy! She is fabulous, fierce and funny as all hell. I like to think I get my cynical sentiment and smart ass mouth from her. I have the letters my grandfather wrote my grandmother while he was away in the service. Along with those letters I have letters from my aunt Lucy who was 16 at the time and wrote my grandmother too. In her letters she treated my grandmother as if she was a best friend that she just hadn't met yet. I loved my aunt Lucy for that too. Here's the sauce....

## My Favorite Aunt Lucy's July 4th Sauce

1 bottle of Hickory Smoke BBQ sauce
   (heavy load use 2 bottles)
1 big bottle of Red's Hot Sauce
1 Cup of French's Mustard

4 Dashes Red Pepper seeds
Hints of; onion powder / garlic powder
Keep stirring & Mix & Taste to liking

My favorite memories eating dinner consist of my uncle watching me eat. I would catch him as I was devouring whatever my grandmother and mother had cheffed up. My uncle Junny would say things like "dang Megan you haven't spoken a word since you sat down with your plate." I'd roll my eyes and continue chewing, it was moments when he completely stopped and stared at me until I paid attention. When I would catch him sitting hand to chin watching my jaws work the deliciousness that's when we would buss out laughing. It was like he admired the way I appreciated each meal and I secretly enjoyed him bringing attention to my love for food.

Another fond memory of good family dinner would be of homemade Boboli pizza nights. Who remembers TGIF Fridays with the Step by Step and Family Matters line up? I remember watching the shows and decorating pizza with olives, onions, peppers, pepperoni and sausage. My mom was the best at making these dinners' fun and fast on a Friday. Unfortunately there are no recipes for pizza in this book and I don't think they make Boboli pizza anymore but just to remind you readers and cookers of the importance of dinners amongst family; Here are my favorite family meals...

Megan Lyon

# Oven baked duck

I favor my Duck cut up into pieces but you can also roast your duck whole if you like! Put oven temperature to 350 degrees and Roast duck in preheated oven for 1 hour.

Cut up (5 pound) whole duck

Place in bowl with ½ cup melted butter and season with 2 teaspoons of Orange Marmalade, Garlic powder, ground pepper, kosher sea salt and Chili Powder.

Place duck pieces spread around in long pan in soaked in 2 quarts chicken broth

Let Duck begin to roast and take intervals of 10-15 min and add drizzle seasoned olive oil on duck (honey, cayenne pepper, kosher sea salt, garlic powder and Sazon)

# Okra and Potatoes

This is a Family favorite.

Cut up your okra and season it with kosher sea salt, garlic powder and ground pepper. Throw the okra in a plastic bag of seasoned flour. (Flour w/ parsley, cayenne pepper, garlic powder and onion powder)

In a separate frying pan make your potatoes just like my home fries in the beginning for breakfast. Just make sure they are low key frying because once you can see your potatoes are softening you add a hint of oil and add the floured okras from the plastic bag.

(Fry/ Brown Okra and Potatoes to your liking)

# My Mother Marla's Enchiladas

Stir fry 2lbs of ground turkey or beef in a frying pan. Add 2 tablespoons of Cuminos, 6 table spoons of chili powder, 2 table spoons of cilantro, 1 tablespoon paprika, add salt and pepper. Chop 2 onions, 1 large can of chopped tomatoes, 2 small cans of green chilies.

Grate 2lbs of Extra Sharp cheddar cheese. (Hold 1 onion to the side with cheese)

After meat is cooked with seasoning and onions to taste. Roll meat in corn tortilla shells, layering onions and cheese in, around and on top of rolled tortilla shells.

# A FEW OF MY FAVORITE DESSERTS

My favorite dessert in the world are my grandmother's cookies. Louella is my grandmother's mother, Louella's Texas tea cakes are the cookies. Granny made these cookies about 3 times a year and when she did she made enough to last for months. Millions of cookies cut with an open carnation milk can. Granny would fill five to six of those tall popcorn cans with teacake cookies. They are called tea cakes from their size and density. The cookie's texture softens as you dip it into tea. My grandmother is from the small historic town of Bastrop Texas, her mother LouElla taught her how to bake these cookies. My Granny then taught my mom and all of us how to make the cookies. Louellas Texas teacakes made the holidays whole with a whole lotta baking going on in the kitchen. Here's the recipe...

# Lou Ella's Texas Tea cakes

6 Cups of Sugar
12 eggs (whole Dozen)
3 cups of shortening

4 teaspoons of baking powder, vanilla
   flavoring, nutmeg and cinnamon
3 tablespoons of Carnation milk
(Use 1 cup for softer cookies)

Add flour to create texture of cookie dough needed

(Make firm but not hard)

My grandmother's name was Desta. I only have one sister Desta and I had to give her a place in my favorite things cookbook because she too is one of my favorite things. So here's her special Chocolate Chip Cookie recipe she came up with, one of the million times we lived together;

# Chocolate Chip Pretzel Cookies

(Another Pillsbury item)

Place the chocolate chip cookie dough you need in a bowl. In a separate bowl crunch and crumble salted pretzels. Mix pretzels with chocolate chip cookie dough. Bake to your liking with oven on 350 degrees.

# A FEW OF MY FAVORITE DRINKS

I was what you call a binge drinker, didn't know my limits and would throw up every time I went out drinking. It took me a while to control my desire to over intake alcohol. It wasn't until I completed my Bartending license and Tips Certification at Manayunk Bartending School that I learned to finally manage my alcohol. I remember one night coming home drunk to Woodbine Ave I was sleeping in the middle room top bunk bed. It must have been too much to climb up that night because I threw up all over the bottom bunk and all over my little brother sleeping in the bottom bunk.

I remember so many nights telling my sister or friends to pull over so I can regurgitate all the vodka and cranberries of the night. With due time I got it together and stopped throwing up on everything and everybody but like I said once I obtained my Bartending license I was straight. It takes one hour to allow one jig of hard liquor, 5 oz. of wine, or 2 beers to leave your system. So here are some of my favorite drinks that I have created over my years of NOT binge drinking....

# My Real Sexy Suede Square Sangria

Bottle of Red or White Sangria
2 Orange slices diced into fours
Lemon slices diced into fours
Lime slices diced into fours
Strawberries sliced in half
½ small container of Blueberries
¼ cup of Sugar
5-8 Jigs of Vodka
2-5 Jigs of Pineapple Rum
(Splash with Ginger Ale to taste)

# The Shakoya Champagne

Bottle of Champagne
10 Jigs of Vodka
5 Jigs of St. Germaine
Mix all together in punch bowl
(Add fruits for flavors of your choice)

# Frick and Frappuccino Eggnog

½ Bottle Starbucks Frappuccino
4 Jigs of Rumchata
3 Jigs of Honey jack Daniels Whiskey
1 Cup of Regular Eggnog
1 Cup of Pennsylvania Dutch Eggnog

# Henny Brandi Cocktail

Combine pineapple and lime juice in cup
Splash of Orange bitters
Add 5 jigs of Hennessy
Top off with Champagne

# FUN FOOD FACTS
# FOR APPENDIX

My favorite type of non-alcoholic drink is seltzer water and different infused waters. Adding a lime, orange and lemon to your water can help with immunity and heartburn. Adding cucumber lemon and lime to your water helps with hydration and appetite control. Both water infusions help your body with digestion.

The combination of any omelet, with the home fries and apple tarts create a complete full size breakfast like no other! Lock you down a man with that combo ladies!

Funny how life goes full circle my siblings and I played up Saint Josephs University track like it was in our back yard and in 2016 I got the pleasure of getting my Masters degree from Saint Josephs too.

Sometimes it's better to cook your bacon in the oven instead of on top of the stove depending on how much time you have to cook breakfast. I learned that from my little cousin Jaser, he's my favorite cousin on my Dad's side. His love for Starbucks inspired the Frick and Frappuccino Eggnog.

My Favorite things to Fry are Fried Zucchini/ Fried Green tomatoes/ Fried Pickles and Fried Eggplant.

For more of my poetry better than the salad poem; Go Buy my first book An Eye for Life Poetry book (2011). You can purchase An Eye for Life Poetry on Xlibris.com, Amazon and Barnes and Noble now!

The last kale salad inspired by Sharifa tastes best after letting it sit overnight in the fridge and eating it the next day. My Granny was best friends with Sharifa's mom and now I'm best friends with Sharifa's daughter.

My Best Friend Alex is now a chef herself cooking for her own company named KC's Kitchen located in West Philly.

This is my brother Noel, he's an artist now but he used to be a Sous-chef for The Franklin Institute's Frog Commissary restaurant, he can cook steak and lobster better than anyone I know!

Drinking is my favorite sport, that's why there's a liquor section in this book! All the drinks in my book are named after some of my great Friends, if you know you know!

My deviled egg filling can also be used to fill little peppers which creates a delicious fresh crisp to devour with the savory yellow paste filling.

The 7 layered Dip is best put together in a big clear glass bowl to see all the different colors come together. It's a $35 dip to make but will feed a party until it ends!

I really looked for my Aunt Lucy's BBQ sauce every summer! The recipe is really my Aunt Eva's, R.I.P. to my Aunt Eva. Thanks to another favorite cousin Kwanè I can share the recipe.

My favorite form of cooking is grilling! I will be on the grill all year round and even in the rain or snow.

The best Methods of Frying are with the air fryer first, then over the stove large pan wide not deep high heat less than 5 minutes of frying.

I came up with the Grilled shrimp Caesar Salad combo from taking my niece Jada and little cousin Josiah to Chuckie Cheese all the time.

Eat a balance of color of foods; Red foods are good for your heart, white foods are good for your immunity, yellow foods are good for your skin, orange foods are good for inflammation, green foods are good for cleansing and purple foods are good for antioxidants.

Printed in the United States
by Baker & Taylor Publisher Services